Hippocrene
CHILDREN'S
ILLUSTRATED
ARABIC
DICTIONARY

ENGLISH · ARABIC
ARABIC · ENGLISH

Compiled and translated by the Editors of Hippocrene Books

Interior illustrations by S. Grant (24, 81, 88); J. Gress (page 10, 21, 24, 37, 46, 54, 59, 65, 72, 75, 77);
K. Migliorelli (page 13, 14, 18, 19, 20, 21, 22, 25, 31, 32, 37, 39, 40, 46, 47, 66, 71, 75, 76, 82, 86, 87);
B. Swidzinska (page 9, 11, 12, 13, 14, 16, 23, 27, 28, 30, 32, 33, 35, 37, 38, 41, 42, 45, 46, 47, 48, 49, 50, 52,
53, 56, 57, 58, 59, 60, 61, 62, 63, 66, 68, 69, 70, 71, 72, 73, 75, 77, 78, 79, 83), N. Zhukov (page 8, 13, 14,
17, 18, 23, 27, 29, 33, 34, 39, 40, 41, 52, 64, 65, 71, 72, 73, 78, 84, 86, 88).

Design, prepress, and production: Graafiset International, Inc.

Cataloging-in-Publication Data available from the Library of Congress.

ISBN 0-7818-0709-3

Printed in Hong Kong.

For information, address:
Hippocrene Books, Inc.
171 Madison Avenue
New York, NY 10016

INTRODUCTION

With their absorbent minds, infinite curiosities and excellent memories, children have enormous capacities to master many languages. All they need is exposure and encouragement.

The easiest way to learn a foreign language is to simulate the same natural method by which a child learns English. The natural technique is built on the concept that language is representational of concrete objects and ideas. The use of pictures and words are the natural way for children to begin to acquire a new language.

The concept of this Illustrated Dictionary is to allow children to build vocabulary and initial competency naturally. Looking at the pictorial content of the Dictionary and saying and matching the words in connection to the drawings gives children the opportunity to discover the foreign language and thus, a new way to communicate.

The drawings in the Dictionary are designed to capture children's imaginations and make the learning process interesting and entertaining, as children return to a word and picture repeatedly until they begin to recognize it.

The beautiful images and clear presentation make this dictionary a wonderful tool for unlocking your child's multilingual potential.

Deborah Dumont, M.A., M.Ed.,
Child Psychologist and Educational Consultant

Arabic Pronunciation

Letter		Pronunciation system used
ا	alif	**aa** like in English 'had' when used as a vowel
ب	baa	**b** as in English 'bent'
ت	taa	**t** as in English 'today'
ث	thaa	**th** like the *th* in English 'think'
ج	jiim	**j** as in English 'just'
ح	Haa	**H** an emphatic *h* pronounced with a strong expulsion of air from the chest
خ	khaa	**kh** like the guttural *ch* in the Scottish pronunciation of 'loch' but more from the throat
د	daal	**d** as in English 'day'
ذ	dhaal	**dh** like the *th* in English 'this'
ر	raa	**r** a rolled *r*
ز	zain	**z** like the *z* in English 'zebra'
س	siin	**s** like the hissing *s* in English 'beside'
ش	shiin	**sh** as in English 'ship'
ص	Saad	**S** an emphatic *s* formed by placing the tongue against the lower palate instead of against the teeth
ض	Daad	**D** an emphatic *d* formed by placing the tongue against the lower palate instead of against the teeth
ط	Taa	**T** an emphatic *t* formed by placing the tongue against the lower palate instead of against the teeth
ظ	Zaa	**Z** an emphatic *z* formed by placing the tongue against the lower palate instead of against the teeth
ع	Ain	**'** a very strong guttural sound produced by compression of the throat and expulsion of the breath

Letter		Pronunciation system used
غ	Ghain	**gh** an exaggerated gargling, uvular r-sound formed by pressing the tongue against the lower palate
ف	faa	**f** as in English 'fire'
ق	qaaf	**q** a k-sound produced in the throat somewhat behind the *c* in English 'cool'
ك	kaaf	**k** as in English 'key'
ل	laam	**l** as in English 'land'
م	miim	**m** as in English 'man'
ن	nuun	**n** as in English 'no'
ه	haa	**h** as in English 'hand'
و	waw	**w** as in English 'wet' when used as a consonant **oo** as in English 'boot' when used as a vowel
ي	yaa	**y** as in English 'yesterday' when used as a consonant **ee** as in English 'see' when used as a vowel
ة	taa marbooTa	**a** feminine ending of nouns or adjectives
◌َ	fatHa	vowel sign indicating a short *a* like in English 'man'
◌ِ	kasra	vowel sign indicating *i* like in English 'ring'
◌ُ	Damma	vowel sign indicating a short *u* like in English 'book'
◌ْ	sukoon	sign written above a consonant indicating a consonant cluster
◌ّ	shadda	sign indicating the doubling of a consonant
ء	hamza	**'** a click pronounced by a quick compression of the upper part of the throat
◌ٍ	tanween	**un/in/an** three signs used to define the end of nouns and adjectives

airplane طائِرَة

Taa-'ira

alligator قاطُور

qaa-Toor

alphabet أَبْجَدِيَّة

ab-ja-diy-ya

antelope ظَبي

Za-bee

antlers قَرنُ الوَعِل

qar-nul wa-eel

apple   تُفَّاحَة

tuf-faa-Ha

aquarium   حَوْضُ الأَسْمَاك

Haw-Dul as-maak

arch   قَنْطَرَة

qan-Ta-ra

arrow   سَهْم

sahm

autumn   خَرِيف

kha-reef

baby طِفْلُ رَضيع

Tif-lun ra-Dee'

backpack شَنْطَةُ ظَهْر

shan-Ta-tu Zahr

badger غُرَيْر

ghu-rair

baker خَبَّاز

khab-baaz

ball كُرَة

ku-ra

balloon بالُون

baa-lon

banana مَوْزَة

maw-za

barley شَعِير

sha'-eer

barrel بِرْميل

bir-meel

basket سَلَّة

sal-la

bat خُفَّاش

khuf-faash

beach شاطِىء

shaa-Ti'

bear دُبّ

dubb

beaver قُنْدُس

qun-dus

bed سَرِير

sa-reer

bee نَحْلَة

naH-la

beetle خُنْفُساء

khun-fu-saa'

bell جَرَس

ja-ras

belt   حِزَام

Hi-zaam

bench   بَنْك

bank

bicycle   دَرَّاجَة

dar-raa-ja

binoculars   مِنْظار

min-Zaar

bird   طَيْر

Tair

birdcage   قَفَص

qa-faS

black   أَسْوَد

as-wad

blocks   قَوَالِبُ البِنَاء

qa-waa-li-bul bi-naa'

blossom   نَوْر

nawr

blue   أَزْرَق

az-rak

boat   قَارِب

qaa-rib

bone   عَظْم

'aZm

book كِتَاب

ki-taab

boot حِذَاء عَالي السَاق

Hi-dhaa' 'aa-leel saaq

bottle زُجَاجَة

zu-jaa-ja

bowl سُلْطانِيَّة

sul-Taa-niy-ya

boy وَلَد

wa-lad

bracelet سِوَار

si-waar

branch

غُصْن

ghuSn

bread

خُبْز

khubz

breakfast

فَطُور

fa-Toor

bridge

جِسْر

jisr

broom

مِكْنَسَة

mik-na-sa

brother

أَخ

akh

brown   أَسْمَر

as-mar

brush   فُرْشَاة

fur-shaat

bucket   دَلْو

dalu

bulletin board   لَوْحَةُ الإِعْلانَات

law-Ha-tul i'-laa-naat

bumblebee   نَحْلَةٌ كَبِيرَة طَنَّانة

naH-la-tun ka-bee-ra Tan-naa-na

butterfly   فَرَاشَة

fa-raa-sha

cab تَاكْسِي

taak-see

cabbage كُرُنْب/مَلْفُوف

ku-runb/mal-foof

cactus صُبَّيْر

Sub-bayr

café مَقْهَى

maq-ha

cake تُورْتَة/كَعْكة

toor-ta/ka'-ka

camel جَمَل

ja-mal

camera

كامِيرَا

kaa-mee-ra

candle

شَمْعَة

sham-'a

candy

بُونْبُون/مُلَبَّس

boon-boon/mu-lab-bas

canoe

قَارِبُ هِنْدِيّ

qaa-ri-bun hin-diy

cap

طَاقِيَّة

Taa-qiy-ya

captain

قُبْطان

qub-Taan

car سَيَّارَة

say-yaa-ra

card وَرَقُ اللَعِب

wa-ra-qul la-'ib

carpet سَجَّادَة

saj-jaa-da

carrot جَزَرَة

ja-za-ra

(to) carry حَمَلَ

Ha-ma-la

castle قَصْر

qaSr

cat قِطَّة

qiT-Ta

cave كَهْف

kahf

chair كُرْسِيّ

kur-siy

cheese جُبْن

jubn

cherry كَرَز

ka-raz

chimney مَدْخَنَة

mad-kha-na

chocolate شُوكُولاتَه

shoo-koo-laa-ta

Christmas tree شَجَرَةُ عِيدِ المِيلاد

sha-ja-ra-tu 'eedil mee-laad

circus سِيرْك

seerk

(to) climb تَسَلَّقَ

ta-sal-la-qa

cloud سَحَاب

sa-Haab

clown مُهَرِّج

mu-har-rij

coach

عَرَبَة

'a-ra-ba

coat

مِعْطَف

mi'-Taf

coconut

جَوْزُ الهِنْد

jaw-zul hind

comb

مِشْط

mishT

comforter

لِحَاف

li-Haaf

compass

بُوْصِلَة

baw-Su-la

(to) cook طَبَخَ

Ta-ba-kha

cork فَلِّينَة

fal-lee-na

corn ذُرَة

dhu-ra

cow بَقَرَة

ba-qa-ra

cracker بَسْكَوِيت

bas-ka-weet

cradle مَهْد

mahd

Cc

(to) crawl   زَحَفَ

za-Ha-fa

(to) cross   عَبَرَ

'a-ba-ra

crown   تاج

taaj

(to) cry   بَكَى

ba-ka

cucumber   خِيَار

khi-yaar

curtain   سِتَارَة

si-taa-ra

(to) dance   رَقَصَ

ra-qa-Sa

dandelion   طَرَخْشَقُون

Ta-rakh-sha-qoon

date   تارِيخ

taa-reekh

deer   أَيِّل

ay-yil

desert   صَحْراء

SaH-raa'

desk   مَكْتَب

mak-tab

dirty   قَذِر

qa-dhir

dog

كَلْب

kalb

doghouse　كُشْكُ الكَلْب

kush-kul kalb

doll　عَرُوسَة

'a-roo-sa

dollhouse　بَيْتُ العَرُوسَة

bayt-tul 'a-roo-sa

dolphin　دُلْفِين

dol-feen

donkey　حِمَار

Hi-maar

dragon　تِنِّين

tin-neen

dragonfly   سُرْمان

sur-maan

(to) draw   رَسَمَ

ra-sa-ma

dress   فُسْتان

fus-taan

(to) drink   شَرِبَ

sha-ri-ba

drum   طَبْل

Tabl

duck   بَطّ

baTT

eagle   نَسْر

nasr

(to) eat   أَكَلَ

a-ka-la

egg   بَيْض

baiD

eggplant   باذِنْجان

baa-dhin-jaan

eight   ثَمَانِيَة

tha-maa-ni-ya

elbow   كُوْع

koo'

elephant   فِيْل

feel

empty

فارِغ

faa-righ

engine

قاطِرَة

qaa-Ti-ra

envelope

ظَرْف

Zarf

escalator

سُلَّمُ مُتَحَرِّك

sul-la-mun mu-ta-Har-rik

Eskimo

أَسْكيمو

as-ki-mo

(to) explore

اِسْتَكْشَفَ

is-tak-sha-fa

eye

عَيْن

'ain

face   وَجْه
wajh

fan   مِرْوَحَة
mir-wa-Ha

father   أَب
ab

fear   خَوْف
khawf

feather   رِيشَة
ree-sha

(to) feed   عَلَفَ
'a-la-fa

fence سُور

soor

fern خِنْشار

khin-shaar

field حَقْل

Haql

field mouse فَأْرُ بَرِّيّ

fa-'run bar-riy

finger إِصْبَع

iS-ba'

fir tree شَجَرَةُ التَّنُّوب

sha-ja-ra-tul tan-noob

fire   نار

naar

fish   سَمَكَة

sa-ma-ka

(to) fish   اِصْطادَ

is-Taa-da

fist   قَبْضَةُ اليَد

qab-Da-tul yad

five   خَمْسَة

kham-sa

flag   عَلَم

'a-lam

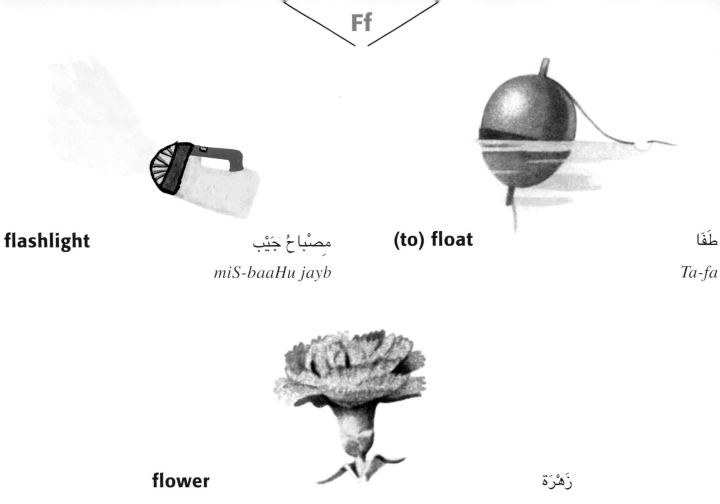

flashlight   مِصْباحُ جَيْب

miS-baaHu jayb

(to) float   طَفَا

Ta-fa

flower   زَهْرَة

zah-ra

(to) fly   طارَ

Taa-ra

foot   قَدَم

qa-dam

fork   شَوْكَة

shaw-ka

fountain   نافُورَة

naa-foo-ra

four

أَرْبَعَة

ar-ba-'a

fox

ثَعْلَب

tha'-lab

frame

بِرْواز

bir-waaz

friend

صَدِيق

Sa-deeq

frog

ضِفْدِعَة

Dif-di-'a

fruit

فاكِهَة

faa-ki-ha

furniture

أَثَاث

a-thaath

garden حَدِيقَة

Ha-dee-qa

gate بَوَّابَة

baw-waa-ba

(to) gather جَمَعَ

ja-ma-'a

geranium غُرْنُوقِيّ

ghur-nu-qiy

giraffe زَرَافَة

za-raa-fa

girl بِنْت

bint

(to) give　　　أَعْطَى

a'-Ta

glass　　　كَأُس

ka's

glasses　　　نَظَّارَة

naZ-Zaa-ra

globe　　　الكُرَة الأَرْضِيَّة

al-ku-ral ar-Diy-ya

glove　　　قُفَّاز

quf-faaz

goat　　　مِعْزَى

mi'-za

goldfish

سَمَكُ ذَهَبِيّ

sa-makun dha-ha-biy

"Good Night"

لَيْلَة سَعِيدَة

lai-la sa'ee-da

"Good-bye"

مَعَ السَلامَة

ma'as sa-laa-ma

goose

وَزَّة

waz-za

grandfather

جَدّ

jadd

grandmother

جَدَّة

jad-da

grapes

عِنَب

'i-nab

grasshopper

جُنْدُب

jun-dub

green

أَخْضَر

akh-Dar

greenhouse

بَيْتٌ زُجَاجِيّ

bay-tun zu-jaa-jiy

guitar

قِيثَارَة

qi-thaa-ra

hammer

مِطْرَقة

miT-ra-qa

hammock

أُرْجُوحَةٌ شَبَكِيَّة

ur-ju-Ha-tun sha-ba-kiy-ya

hamster

هَمْسْتِر

hams-ter

hand

يَد

yad

handbag

حَقِيبَةُ يَد

Ha-qi-ba-tu yad

handkerchief

مَنْديل

mand-deel

harvest حَصْد

HaSd

hat قُبَّعَة

qub-ba-'a

hay تِبْن

tibn

headdress زِيْنَةٌ للرَّأْس

zai-na-tun lil-ra's

heart قَلْب

qalb

hedgehog قُنْفُذ

qun-fudh

hen دَجَاجَة

da-jaa-ja

(to) hide اِحْتَبَأ

ikh-ta-ba'a

highway طَرِيقٌ عام

Ta-ree-qun 'aam

honey عَسَل

'asal

horns قُرُون

qu-roon

horse حِصَان

Hi-Saan

horseshoe

حَدْوَة

Had-wa

hourglass

ساعَةٌ رَمْلِيَّة

saa-'a-tun ram-liy-ya

house

بَيْت

bayt

(to) hug

اِحْتَضَنَ

iH-ta-Da-na

hydrant

مِضَخَةُ الحَرِيق

mi-Da-kha-tul Ha-reeq

ice cream

جيْلاَتي/بوُظَة

ge-laat-ti/boo-Za

ice cubes

مُكَعَّباتُ ثَلْج

mu-ka'-'a-baa-tu thalj

ice-skating

تَزَلُّج عَلَى الجَليد

ta-zal-luj 'alal ja-leed

instrument

اَلَةٌ مُوسيِقيَّة

aa-la-tun moo-see-qiy-ya

iris

سَوْسَن

saw-san

iron

مِكْواة

mik-waat

island

جَزيرَة

ja-zee-ra

jacket جاكِيت

jaa-ket

jam مُرَبَّى

mu-rab-ba

jigsaw puzzle أَحْجِيَةُ الصُوَر المَقْطُوعَة

aH-ji-ya-tul Su-war al-maq-Tu'a

jockey جُوكِي

jo-kee

juggler بَهْلَوَان

bah-la-waan

(to) jump قَفَزَ

qa-fa-za

kangaroo   كَنْغَر

kan-ghar

key   مِفْتاح

mif-taaH

kitten   قُطَيْطَة

qu-Tay-Ta

knife   سِكِّين

sik-keen

knight   فارِس

faa-ris

(to) knit   حَبَكَ

Ha-ba-ka

knot   عُقْدَة

'uq-da

koala bear   الكُوال

al-ko-waal

ladder سُلَّم

sul-lam

ladybug دُعْسُوقَة

du'-su-qa

lamb حَمَل

Ha-mal

lamp مِصْباح

mis-baaH

(to) lap لَحَسَ

la-Ha-sa

laughter ضَحَك

Da-Hik

lavender   خُزَامَى

khu-zaa-ma

lawn mower   مِحَشّ

mi-Hash

leaf   وَرَقَة

wa-ra-qa

leg   رِجْل

rijl

lemon   لَيْمُون

lay-moon

lettuce   خَسّ

khass

lightbulb لَمْبَةٌ كَهْرَبائِيَّة

lam-ba-tun kah-ra-baa-iy-ya

lighthouse مَنَارَة

ma-naa-ra

lilac لَيْلَك

lay-lak

lion أَسَد

a-saḍ

(to) listen اِسْتَمَعَ

is-ta-ma-'a

lobster كَرْكَنْد

kar-kand

lock

كَالُون

kaa-loon

lovebird

البَبَّغَاءُ المُتَيَّمَة

al-bab-ba-ghaa-'ul mu-tay-ya-ma

luggage

أَمْتِعَة

am-ti-'a

lumberjack

حَطَّاب

HaT-Taab

lunch

غَدَاء

gha-daa'

lynx

وَشَق

wa-shaq

magazine　　مَجَلَّة

ma-jal-la

magician　　ساحِر

saa-Hir

magnet　　مَغْنَطِيس

magh-na-Tees

map　　خَرِيطَة

kha-ree-Ta

maple leaf　　وَرْقَةُ القَيْقَب

wa-ra-qa-tul qay-qab

marketplace　　ساحَةُ السُوْق

saa-Ha-tul sooq

mask　　قِنَاع

qi-naa'

messy

غَيْر مُرَتَّب

ghair mu-rat-tab

milkman

بائِعُ الحَلِيب

baa-ee-'ul Haleeb

mirror

مِرْآة

mir-aat

mitten

كَفٌّ بِلا أَصابِع

kaf-fun bi-laa a-Saa-bi'

money

نُقُود

nu-qood

monkey

قِرْد

qird

moon

قَمَر

qa-mar

Mm

mother أُم
umm

mountain جَبَل
ja-bal

mouse فَأُر
fa'r

mouth فَم
fam

mushroom فُطْر
fu-Tr

music مُوسِيقَى
moo-see-qa

naked عُرْيان
'ur-yaan

necklace عِقْد
'iqd

needle إِبْرَة
ib-ra

nest عُشّ
'ush

newspaper جَرِيدَة
ja-ree-da

nightingale   بُلْبُل

bul-bul

nine   تِسْعَة

tis-'a

notebook   دَفْتَر

daf-tar

number   عَدَد

'a-dad

nut   جَوْز

jawz

oar

مِجْذاف

mij-dhaaf

ocean liner

سَفينَة

sa-fee-na

old

عَجُوز

'a-jooz

1

one

واحِد

waa-Hid

onion

بَصَل

ba-Sal

open

مَفْتُوح

maf-TooH

orange

بُرْتُقَال

bur-tu-qaal

ostrich

نَعَامَة

na-'aa-ma

owl

بُوْمَة

boo-ma

ox

ثَوْر

thawr

padlock   قُفْل

qufl

paint   دِهَان

di-haan

painter

رَسَّام

ras-saam

pajamas   بِيجَامَة

bee-jaa-ma

palm tree   نَخْلَة

nakh-la

paper   وَرَقَة

wa-ra-qa

parachute   مِظلَّةُ هُبُوط

mi-Zal-latu hu-booT

park

مُنْتَزَه

mun-ta-zah

parrot

بَبَّغَاء

ba-ba-ghaa'

passport

جَوَازُ سَفَر

ja-waa-zu sa-far

patch

رُقْعَة

ruq-'a

path

مَمَرّ

ma-marr

peach

خَوْخ/دُرَّاق

khawkh/dur-raaq

pear

كُمَّثْرَى/إِجَّاص

kum-math-ra/eej-jaas

pebble

حَصَاة

Ha-Saat

(to) peck

نَقَرَ

na-qa-ra

(to) peel

قَشَّرَ

qa-sha-ra

pelican

بَجَع

ba-ja'

pencil

قَلَم

qa-lam

penguin

بِطْرِيق

biT-reeq

people

ناس

naas

piano   بِيَانُو

bi-yaa-noo

pickle   مُخَلَّل

mu-khal-lal

pie   فَطِيرَة

fa-Tee-ra

pig   خِنْزِير

khin-zeer

pigeon   حَمَام

Ha-maam

pillow   وِسَادَة

wi-saa-da

pin   دَبُّوس

dab-boos

pine

صَنَوْبَر

Sa-naw-bar

pineapple

أَنَانَاس

a-naa-naas

pit

نَوَاة

na-waat

pitcher

إِبْرِيق

ib-reeq

plate

صَحْن

SaHn

platypus

مِنْقَارُ البَطَّة

min-qaa-rul baT-Ta

(to) play

لَعَبَ

la-'a-ba

plum

بُرْقُوق/خَوْخ

bur-qooq/khawkh

polar bear

دُبٌّ قُطْبِيّ

dub-bun quT-biy

pony

فَرَسُ قَزَم

fa-ra-sun qa-zam

pot

حَلَّة/طَنْجَرَة

Hal-la/Tan-ja-ra

potato

بَطَاطِس/بَطَاطَا

ba-Taa-Tis/ba-Taa-Ta

(to) pour سَكَبَ

sa-ka-ba

present هَدِيَّة

ha-diy-ya

(to) pull شَدَّ

shad-da

pumpkin قَرْع

qar'

Qq

puppy جَرْو

ja-roo

queen مَلِكَة

ma-li-ka

rabbit

أَرْنَب

ar-nab

raccoon

راكُون

raa-koon

racket

مِضْرَب

miD-rab

radio

رادْيُو

raad-yo

radish

فُجْل

fujl

raft   رَمَث

ra-math

rain   مَطَر

ma-Tar

rainbow   قَوْسُ قُزَح

qaw-su qu-zaH

raincoat   مِعْطَفٌ ضِدّ المَطَر

mi'-Ta-fun Didd al-ma-Tar

raspberry   تُوْتُ شَوْكِيّ

too-tun shaw-kiy

(to) read

قَرَأ

qa-ra-'a

red

أَحْمَر

aHmar

refrigerator

ثَلّاجَة

thal-laa-ja

rhinoceros

كَرْكَدَنّ

kar-ka-dann

ring

خاتِم

khaa-tim

(to) ring   دَقَّ الجَرَس

daq-qal ja-ras

river   نَهْر

nahr

road   طَرِيق

Ta-reeq

rocket   صارُوخ

Saa-rookh

roof   سَطْحُ البَيْت

saT-Hul bayt

rooster   دِيك

deek

root   جِذْر
ji-dhr

rope   حَبْل
Habl

rose   وَرْدَة
war-da

(to) row   جَذَفَ
ja-dha-fa

ruler   مِسْطَرَة
mis-Ta-ra

(to) run   رَكَضَ
ra-ka-Da

safety pin   دَبُّوسُ الأمَان

dab-boo-sul a-maan

(to) sail   أَبْحَرَ

ab-Ha-ra

sailor   بَحَّار

baH-Haar

salt   مِلْح

milH

scarf   وِشَاح

wi-shaaH

school   مَدْرَسَة

mad-ra-sa

scissors مِقَصّ

mi-qaSS

screwdriver مِفَكّ

mi-fakk

seagull نَوْرَس

naw-ras

seesaw نَوَّاسَة

naw-waa-sa

seven سَبْعَة

sab-'a

(to) sew خَيَّطَ

khay-ya-Ta

shark قِرْش

qirsh

sheep خَرُوف

kha-roof

shell صَدَفَة

Sa-da-fa

shepherd راعٍ

raa-'een

ship باخِرَة

baa-khi-ra

shirt قَمِيص

qa-meeS

shoe جَزْمَة/حِذَاء

jaz-ma/Hi-dhaa'

shovel مِجْرَفَة

mij-ra-fa

(to) show عَرَضَ

'a-ra-Da

shower دُشّ

dush

shutter شِيْش

sheesh

sick مَرِيض

ma-reeD

sieve   مُنْخُل

mun-khul

(to) sing   غَنَّى

ghan-na

(to) sit   جَلَسَ

ja-la-sa

six   سِتَّة

sit-ta

sled   مِرْلَقَة

miz-la-qa

(to) sleep   نامَ

naa-ma

small   صَغِير

Sa-gheer

smile   اِبْتِسامة

ib-ti-saa-ma

snail   حَلَزُون

Ha-la-zoon

snake   حَيَّة

Hay-ya

snow   ثَلْج

thalj

sock   جَوَارِب/كَلْسات

ja-waa-rib/kal-saat

sofa   أَرِيكَة

a-ree-ka

sparrow   عُصْفُور

'uS-foor

spider   عَنْكَبُوت

'an-ka-boot

spiderweb   بَيْتُ العَنْكَبُوت

bay-tul 'an-ka-boot

spoon   مِلْعَقَة

mil-'a-qa

squirrel   سِنْجاب

sin-jaab

stairs

دَرَج

dar-raj

stamp

طابَعٌ بَريدِيّ

Taa-ba-'un ba-ree-diy

starfish

نَجْمُ البَحْر

naj-mul baHr

stork

لَقْلَق

laq-laq

stove

مَوْقِد

maw-qid

strawberry

فَرَاوْلَة/فريز

fa-raaw-la/fraiz

subway

مِتْرُو نَفَقِيّ

mi-troo na-fa-qiy

sugar cube مُكَعَّبُ سُكَّر

mu-qaʻ-ʻabu suk-kar

sun شَمْس

shams

sunflower عَبَّادُ الشَّمْس

ʻab-baa-dul shams

sweater سِتْرَة

sit-ra

(to) sweep كَنَسَ

ka-na-sa

swing أُرْجُوحَة

ur-ju-Ha

table

مائِدَة

ma-'i-da

teapot

إِبْرِيقُ الشَّاي

ib-ree-qul shaay

teddy bear

دُبٌّ قُمَاشِيّ

dub-bun qu-maa-shiy

television

تِلِفِزْيُون

ti-li-fiz-yoon

ten

عَشَرَة

'a-sha-ra

tent

خَيْمَة

khay-ma

theater مَسْرَح

maS-raH

thimble كُشْتُبَان

kush-tu-baan

(to) think فَكَّرَ

fak-ka-ra

3

three ثَلاثَة

tha-laa-tha

tie كَرافات

kraa-faat

(to) tie رَبَطَ

ra-ba-Ta

tiger نِمْر

nimr

toaster مِحْمَصَةُ خُبْزٍ كَهْرَبائِيَّة

miH-ma-Sa-tu khub-zin kah-ra-baa-iy-ya

tomato طَمَاطِم/بَنَدُورَة

Ta-maa-tim/ba-na-doo-ra

toucan طُوقان

too-qaan

towel فُوْطَة

foo-Ta

tower بُرْج

burj

toy box

عُلْبَةُ اللُّعَب

'ul-ba-tul lu-'ab

tracks

خُطُوطُ السِّكَّة الحَدِيدِيَّة

khu-Too-tul sik-kal Ha-dee-diy-ya

train station

مَحَطَّةُ القِطَار

ma-HaT-Ta-tul qi-Taar

tray

صِينِيَّة

See-niy-ya

tree

شَجَرَة

sha-ja-ra

trough

مِعْلَف

mi'-laf

truck

شاحِنَة

shaa-Hi-na

trumpet

بُوْق

booq

tulip

تُولِيب

tu-leep

tunnel

نَفَق

na-faq

turtle

سُلَحْفاة

su-laH-faat

twins

تَوْأَمان

taw-'a-maan

two

إِثْنان

ith-naan

umbrella　　　مِظَلَّة

mi-Zal-la

uphill　　　مُرْتَقَى

mur-ta-qa

Vv

vase　　　زَهْرِيَّة

zah-riy-ya

veil　　　حِجَاب

Hi-jaab

village قَرْيَة

qar-ya

violet بَنَفْسَج

ba-naf-saj

violin كَمَان

ka-maan

voyage رِحْلَة

riH-la

waiter

سُفْرَجِي

suf-ra-ji

(to) wake up

اِسْتَيْقَظَ

is-tay-qa-Za

walrus

فَظ

faZ

(to) wash

غَسَلَ

gha-sa-la

watch

ساعَة

saa-'a

(to) watch

راقَبَ

raa-qa-ba

(to) water سَقَى

sa-qa

waterfall شَلَّال

sha-laal

watering can مِرَشَّة

mi-rash-sha

watermelon بِطِّيخ

biT-Teekh

weather vane دَوَّارَةُ الهَوَاء

daw-waa-ra-tul ha-waa'

(to) weigh وَزَنَ

wa-za-na

whale　　　حُوْت

Hoot

wheel　　　عَجَلَة

'a-ja-la

wheelbarrow　　　عَرَبَةٌ يَد

'a-ra-ba-tu yad

whiskers　　　شارِبُ الحَيَوَان

shaa-ri-bul Ha-ya-waan

(to) whisper　　　هَمَسَ

ha-ma-sa

whistle　　　صَفَّارَة

Saf-faa-ra

white أَبْيَض

ab-yaD

wig شَعْرُ مُسْتَعار

sha'-run mus-ta-'aar

wind رِيح

reeH

window شُبَّاك

shub-baak

wings أَجْنِحَة

aj-ni-Ha

winter شِتَاء

shi-taa'

wolf

ذِئْب

dhi-'b

wood

خَشَب

kha-shab

word

كَلِمَة

ka-li-ma

(to) write

كَتَبَ

ka-ta-ba

yellow

أَصْفَر

aS-far

Zz

zebra

حِمَارٌ وَحْشِيّ

Hi-maa-run waH-shiy

ت

ب

أ

candle	شَمْعَة
backpack	شَنْطَةُ ظَهْر
fork	شَوْكَة
chocolate	شُوكُولاتَه
shutter	شِيش

ص

rocket	صارُوخ
cactus	صُبَّيْر
desert	صَحْراء
plate	صَحْن
shell	صَدَفَة
friend	صَديق
small	صَغير
whistle	صَفَّارَة
pine	صَنَوْبَر
tray	صينِيَّة

ض

laughter	ضَحِك
frog	ضِفْدَعَة

ط

airplane	طائِرَة
stamp	طابِعُ بَريدِيّ
(to) fly	طارَ
cap	طَاقِيَّة
(to) cook	طَبَخَ

drum	طَبْل
dandelion	طَرَخْشَقُون
road	طَريق
highway	طَريقٌ عام
(to) float	طَفَا
baby	طِفْلُ رَضيع
tomato	طَمَاطِم
pot	طَنْجَرَة
toucan	طُوقان
bird	طَيْر

ظ

antelope	ظَبِي
envelope	ظَرْف

ع

sunflower	عَبَّادُ الشَّمْس
(to) cross	عَبَرَ
wheel	عَجَلَة

old	عَجُوز
number	عَدَد
coach	عَرَبَة
wheelbarrow	عَرَبَةُ يَد
(to) show	عَرَضَ
doll	عَرُوسَة
naked	عُرْيان
honey	عَسَل
nest	عُشّ
ten	عَشَرَة
sparrow	عُصْفُور
bone	عَظْم
necklace	عِقْد
knot	عُقْدَة
toy box	عُلْبَةُ اللُّعَب
(to) feed	عَلَفَ
flag	عَلَم
grapes	عِنَب
spider	عَنْكَبُوت
eye	عَيْن

غ

lunch	غَدَاء
geranium	غُرْنُوقِي
badger	غُرَيْر
(to) wash	غَسَلَ
branch	غُصْن
(to) sing	غَنَّى
messy	غَيْر مُرَتَّب

ف

mouse	فَأْر
field mouse	فَأْرُ بَرِّي
knight	فارِس

English	العربية
	هـ
present	هَدِيَّة
whisper	هَمَسَ
hamster	هَمْستِر
	و
one	واحد
face	وَجْه
rose	وَرْدَة
card	وَرَقُ اللَّعِب
leaf; paper	وَرَقَة
maple leaf	وَرَقَةُ القَيْقَب
goose	وَزَّة
(to) weight	وَزَنَ
pillow	وِسَادَة
scarf	وِشَاح
lynx	وَشَق
boy	وَلَد
	ي
hand	يَد

English	العربية
candy	مُلَبَّس
salt	مِلْح
spoon	مِلْعَقَة
cabbage	مَلْفُوف
queen	مَلِكَة
path	مَمَرّ
lighthouse	مَنَارَة
park	مُنْتَزَه
sieve	مُنْخُل
handkerchief	مَنْدِيل
binoculars	مِنْظَار
platypus	مِنْقَارُ البَطَّة
cradle	مَهْد
clown	مُهَرِّج
banana	مَوْزَة
music	مُوسِيقَى
stove	مَوْقِد
	ن
fire	نار
people	ناس
fountain	نافُورَة
sleep	نامَ
starfish	نَجْمُ البَحْر
bee	نَحْلَة
bumblebee	نَحْلَة كَبِيرَة طَنَّانة
palm tree	نَخْلَة
eagle	نَسْر
glasses	نَظَّارَة
ostrich	نَعَامَة
tunnel	نَفَق
(to) peck	نَقَرَ
money	نُقُود
tiger	نمْر
river	نَهْر
pit	نَوَاة
seesaw	نَوَّاسَة
blossom	نَوْر
seagull	نَوْرَس

English	العربية
oar	مِجْذاف
magazine	مَجَلَّة
lawn mower	مِحَشّ
train station	مَحَطَّةُ القِطَار
toaster	مِحْمَصَةُ خُبْزٍ كَهْرَبائِيّة
pickle	مُخَلَّل
chimney	مِدْخَنَة
school	مَدْرَسَة
mirror	مِرْآة
jam	مُرَبَّى
uphill	مُرْتَقَى
watering can	مِرَشَّة
fan	مِرْوَحَة
sick	مَرِيض
sled	مِزْلَقَة
theater	مَسْرَح
comb	مِشْط
flashlight	مِصْباحُ جَيْب
hydrant	مِضَخَّةُ الحَرِيق
racket	مِضْرَب
rain	مَطَر
hammer	مِطْرَقَة
umbrella	مَظَلَّة
parachute	مَظَلَّةُ هُبُوط
"Good-bye"	مَعَ السَلامَة
goat	مَعْزَى
coat	مِعْطَف
raincoat	مِعْطَفٌ ضِد المَطَر
trough	مِعْلَف
ruler	مِسْطَرَة
magnet	مَغْنَطِيس
lamp	مِصْباح
key	مِفْتاح
open	مَفْتُوح
screwdriver	مِفَكّ
scissors	مِقَصّ
café	مَقْهَى
desk	مَكْتَب
sugar cube	مُكَعَّبُ سُكَّر
ice cubes	مُكَعَّباتُ ثَلْج
broom	مِكْنَسَة
iron	مِكْواة

Tales of Languedoc: From the South of France
Samuel Jacques Brun
For readers of all ages, here is a masterful collection of folk tales from the south of France.
Ages 12 and up
248 pages • 33 b/w sketches • 5 1/2 x 8 1/4 • 0-7818-0715-8 • W • $14.95hc • (793)

Twenty Scottish Tales and Legends
Edited by Cyril Swinson
Illustrated by Allan Stewart
Twenty enchanting stories take the reader to an extraordinary world of magic harps, angry giants, mysterious spells and gallant Knights.
Ages 9 and up
215 pages • 5 1/2 x 8 1/4 • 8 b/w illustrations • 0-7818-0701-8 • W • $14.95 hc • (789)

The Little Mermaid and Other Tales
Hans Christian Andersen
Here is a near replica of the first American edition of 27 classic fairy tales from the masterful Hans Christian Andersen.
Ages 9 and up
508 pages • b/w illustrations • 6 x 9 • 0-7818-0720-4 • W • $19.95hc • (791)

Pakistani Folk Tales: Toontoony Pie and Other Stories
Ashraf Siddiqui and Marilyn Lerch
Illustrated by Jan Fairservis
In these 22 folk tales are found not only the familiar figures of folklore—kings and beautiful princesses—but the magic of the Far East, cunning jackals, and wise holy men.
Ages 7 and up
158 pages • 6 1/2 x 8 1/2 • 38 illustrations • 0-7818-0703-4 • W • $12.50hc • (784)

Folk Tales from Chile
Brenda Hughes
This selection of 15 tales gives a taste of the variety of Chile's rich folklore. Fifteen charming illustrations accompany the text.
Ages 7 and up
121 pages • 5 1/2 x 8 1/4 • 15 illustrations • 0-7818-0712-3 • W • $12.50hc • (785)